Orel Hershiser

"He's a rainy day for the other team."
— Reggie Jackson
PHOTO: Jon Soohoo, Los Angeles Dodgers

I don't know that we will ever again see the likes of what we have seen Orel Hershiser accomplish. It may be that no pitcher in history stayed in the groove for so long and so well.

— Kirk Gibson,
Los Angeles Dodgers
National League MVP, 1988

OREL HERSHISER

<hr>

Up Close and Personal

Bill Horlacher
and
Joe Smalley

Here's Life Publishers

First printing, April 1989

Published by
HERE'S LIFE PUBLISHERS, INC.
P. O. Box 1576
San Bernardino, CA 92402

Library of Congress Catalog Card No. 89-83738.

The material in this booklet has been adapted from material originally published in *Grand Slam* (© 1987, Bill Horlacher and Joe Smalley) and is used by permission.

We gratefully acknowledge the courtesy of the Los Angeles Dodgers in providing photographs for use in this booklet. We sincerely appreciate their cooperation.

Scripture quotations are from *The New American Standard Bible,* © The Lockman Foundation 1960, 1962, 1963, 1968, 1971, 1972, 1975, 1977.

References for the Branch Rickey chapter are: 1. Murray Polner, *Branch Rickey* (New York: Signet, 1982), p. 240; 2. Jules Tygiel, *Baseball's Great Experiment* (New York: Vintage Books, 1984), p. 28; 3. Polner, pp. 39-41; 4. Polner, p. 119; 5. Roger Kahn, *The Boys of Summer* (New York: Signet, 1973), p. 101; 6. Polner, p. 165; 7. Fulton Oursler, "Rookie of the Year," *The Reader's Digest* (February 1948), p. 35; 8. Polner, pp. 166-67; 9. Polner, p. 179; 10. Polner, p. 180; 11. Polner, p. 196; 12. Polner, p. 198; 13. Tygiel, p. 200; 14. Polner, p. 205; 15. Tygiel, p. 343; 16. Polner, p. 60.

Contents

Contents

OREL HERSHISER

Fortunately for the batters, Orel is allowed to pitch only one ball at a time.
PHOTO: Andrew D. Bernstein, Los Angeles Dodgers

**59 Straight Scoreless Innings
Cy Young Award
MVP of World Series**

* * *

**"What should we put on
the T-shirts?"**

Orel Hershiser

"The Best I Can Be"

At first, the T-shirt makers just didn't know what to do. It was obvious they should celebrate Orel Hershiser's 1988 successess in cotton and poly—and make a buck while they were at it.

But which success should they highlight on the shirts? After all, in just one season this Dodger pitcher had set an all-time big league record with his 59 consecutive scoreless innings, had won the Cy Young Award, and had earned selection as Most Valuable Player of the World Series. In addition, he'd put his face on the cover of *Sports Illustrated* as "Sportsman of the Year," outdoing such others as Magic Johnson, Florence Griffith Joyner and Greg Louganis.

What were the T-shirt men to do? There was just too much glory for one hunk of fabric to hold. But then the answer came. "No sweat," said the top guns of the T-shirt industry. "We'll just give the folks their choice."

And so they did. Following in the footsteps of those who brought us 31 flavors and 57 varieties, they offered us three T's in honor of O. "Just mark your choice," said the ad in the *Sporting News* — "Cy Young," "Series MVP," or "59."

Those outside the T-shirt industry were also impressed by Hershiser's great season. Dodger teammate Kirk Gibson just about burst with Orel enthusiasm following L.A.'s World Series win over Oakland: "I don't know that we will ever again see the likes of what we have seen Orel Hershiser accomplish. It may be that no pitcher in history stayed in the groove for so long and so well."

Whew! And Gibson wasn't even selling any T-shirts. Neither was Reggie Jackson, but the former Oakland slugger couldn't

*Hershiser was named Pacific Dining Car
Co-Dodger of the Year–1988.*
PHOTO: Andrew D. Bernstein, Los Angeles Dodgers

resist a little Orel praise during the Series. "Orel Hershiser is the real thing," said Reggie. "He's 24-carat. He's 99-and-44/100 percent pure. He's Ivory Snow. He's Post Toasties. He's a rainy day for the other team."

Suddenly good ol' Orel Leonard Hershiser IV (nicknamed "O" by his parents) was being compared with Hall of Famers like Walter Johnson, Christy Mathewson and Cy Young. And that must have been a nice change for Orel. Owner of a baby face and a skinny frame, he's used to being compared with librarians or accountants.

"Let's face it," he says, "I'm just a pale guy with glasses, long arms and a sunken chest. I look like I never lifted a weight, and like I work in a flour factory. People compare me to Clark Kent and Superman, but Clark Kent had a good body. I'm Jimmy Olsen."

In his youth, Hershiser was even skinnier than now. "Even to get to be anemic looking," wrote *Sports Illustrated,* "Hershiser had to fill out some,"–which he did during the six-month period following his sophomore year in college. "I grew three inches through that summer," recalls Orel, "and gained 20 pounds. All of a sudden, instead of my fastball being 81 or 82 (miles-per-hour), it was now 85 or 86."

The added zip gave O at least minor league, if not major league, ability. So, the Dodgers made him a 17th round draft choice after that junior season. Still, says Orel, "I was more a suspect than a prospect."

The "suspect" was to spend the next five years floundering in the Dodger system. The organization made him a relief pitcher, but that role didn't fit him well. Orel likes to view the game as a whole, setting up hitters from one at-bat to the next. He couldn't do that as a reliever.

The rap on Hershiser in the minors was that he lacked aggressiveness. People judged him by his baby face and not by the man inside. He was actually very intense, a fact shown by his painful frustration in the minors.

Orel especially had trouble forgetting a bad performance. After a loss, he would torment himself with questions like, "Why did I throw that pitch?" or, "Why do I always lose?"

The would-be Dodger tried everything to overcome his frustration. He once even tried washing it away. "I thought I could shower it off," says O. "I took one after the game, then went home and couldn't sleep. I thought, *A nice hot shower will relax me,* so I took another shower and got back into bed, but still couldn't sleep. Then I thought, *Maybe I should take another one, a cold one.* I was always looking for something to get me relaxed because I was so frustrated."

Yes, Orel was one pitcher who really had gone to the showers — but he still needed to be cleansed. And that took place through his friendship with another minor league pitcher, Butch Wickensheimer.

Wickensheimer, says Hershiser (now there's a pair of last names!), was a Christian who liked people for the sake of liking them, not for what he could get in return. O looked up to "Wicks," who was older, and the two ended up rooming together. One day, Wicks asked Orel if he was a Christian, and an interesting dialogue began.

"Yes," answered Hershiser, "I go to church on Christmas and Easter."

"Then you do know who Jesus Christ is," said Wickensheimer.

"Yes, He's the one who died on the cross for our sins and we go to church to worship Him."

"But do you have a personal relationship with Him?"

"No, not really."

The two talked about the meaning of

sin, and Orel began to realize that he was separated from God. No, he wasn't a doper or a drinker, and he didn't play around with sex (something he is thankful for, as we'll see). But, as O learned, sin comes wrapped in a lot of different packages including jealousy, anger, and selfishness.

Still, Hershiser wasn't convinced. In fact, he says he was kind of jealous because Wicks had something he didn't. "I went to Christian meetings with him and read the Bible just to find something to prove it wrong so I didn't have to choose it."

Eventually, though, Orel's attitude changed. "I didn't have the answers for eternity. I really didn't know what was going to happen after death. It came to a point where I knew this was the solution, and I finally bowed and said, 'I believe it, Lord; I know that I'm a sinner. I know that Your plan of salvation is that I must believe in Your Son who died on the cross and rose from the dead, and that if I believe it, I go to heaven.' And I said, 'I accept Your Son right now!' At that moment there were no bangs or whistles or fireworks. But I had peace and security and knew I was going to heaven."

Within two or three months, O did something that perhaps other new believers should consider. As a means of taking a stand for his new faith, he placed himself in a public position of Christian responsibility. "I did that through the organization, Baseball Chapel," he says. "It was in San Antonio (Class AA), and I decided to be a chapel leader because I wanted to stand up for what I believe and be accountable. I became an assistant to the chapel leader; I wouldn't take the actual leadership because I knew I was not strong enough."

But to publicly stand up for Christ, Orel knew he had to privately take care of some past wrongs. One of the first people he talked to was a former teammate. "When I was in A ball," says Hershiser, "I stole a baseball glove out of another guy's locker. He had about five of them, brand new gloves, and I had only one. After I became a Christian, I went back and gave him the glove and said, 'I'm sorry.' "

Orel learned to say "sorry" to God as well, by confessing sin as soon as he became aware of it. "I wouldn't even wait for my prayers at night," he says. "I would just confess at that moment." This habit gave Orel the assurance of being close to God, and it aided his spiritual growth since sin could not gain a foothold in his life for more than a few moments.

O was now playing in the big leagues

*A full house looks on as Orel spends
another "day at the office."*
PHOTO: Andrew D. Bernstein, Los Angeles Dodgers

spiritually, but he still did his pitching from
minor league mounds. He yearned for the
majors, and in 1981 it looked like he might
soon get there. Pitching for San Antonio, O
had an 0.60 earned run average going into
June.

"Everybody thought the Dodgers would
call me up to the big leagues," he recalls. "I
got caught up in the scouting reports, what
I read in the papers and the phone calls from
the Dodgers. I stopped praying and I stopped
listening to God. I started going out with the
guys and not having a focus on what I was
supposed to be doing. And I stopped doing
the things that got me that 0.60 ERA—
things that had given me the peace of mind
I'd had."

The result was brutal. In his next three

outings, Orel gave up 24 earned runs without getting an out! His ERA ballooned to 8.6, and his major league debut was delayed until 1983.

"It was like God had just come down from heaven and hit me over the head and said, 'You dummy. Remember who got you here. Remember what's going on. Remember where your ability came from.' I really believe if God had allowed me to get to the big leagues at that moment, I would have forgotten Him. I would have started thinking, *Orel Hershiser is the one who got me here.*"

No wonder, then, that TV cameras observed Orel singing to himself between innings of his final game victory over the A's in the '88 Series. He wasn't just making music to pass the time away. He was singing hymns to maintain his focus on the God he loves—"Remember who got you here."

Johnny Carson may not completely understand the reason for Hershiser's Series singing, but he must know it was sincere. During an interview on *The Tonight Show*, Johnny suddenly asked Orel to give the audience a sample of what he'd sung. The pitcher bravely accepted Carson's challenge and came up with a pleasing version of the doxology ("Praise God from whom all blessings flow . . . "). It was an unusual moment in the world of network TV, and one that showed both Orel's love for the Lord and his love of life.

Such a combination is not rare for Hershiser. He is determined to be a positive role model for youth. And he's equally determined to show that Christians can have fun — that they need not be baptized in lemon juice.

"At first [soon after he trusted Christ] I thought, *How can I be Christian? I'm not straight enough.* I liked to have fun; I liked to be giddy. But in reading the Bible I discovered there was no contradiction there. If anything, I felt freer after I found Christ, freer to express my emotions, freer to open up to people."

Examples? Try his comment about his skinny body: "I'm the only guy on the Dodgers team who can palm a basketball with his chest." Then there's the autographed photo Orel and his wife Jamie received from Lasorda's pal, Frank Sinatra. Their names were spelled "Oral" and "Jaime." The picture hangs in the Hershisers' den, and Orel notes, "That's from our very close personal friend, Hank Sinatra."

The serious side of Orel shows through clearly also, especially in competition. Already well known is the large amount of time O spends in preparing to pitch, entering information on hitters into his personal computer and studying videotapes of his own delivery. Equally well known are the strengths of Orel's pitching repertoire, his sinking fastball and his vicious curve. But what's not so well known is the effect of his Christian faith on his motivation. Simply put, he feels a responsibility to do his best with his God-given talent.

"Just because you're a Christian does not mean you have to be a wimp," he says. "When I die, I want God to be able to look at a highlight film of my life, and on every clip He pulls out I want Him to see me trying my hardest. Christianity has freed me up because I don't have to worry when I fail. I don't have to worry about tomorrow, because all tomorrow brings is me, and God, and me doing my best with the talent He's given me."

Lasorda gave Orel the nickname "Bulldog" during his rookie year. The name was given to remind him to challenge hitters because he was intimidated by their major league credentials. Today, the nickname is not needed for motivation, but it does describe Orel's strong determination.

Knowing that his talent comes from

God not only spurs Hershiser to give his best, but it also causes him to give credit to the Lord for his success. This was obvious after he struck out Howard Johnson to finish L.A.'s victory over the Mets in the '88 N.L.C.S. Rather than proclaim himself "Number 1," Orel knelt beside the mound for a brief prayer—brief, because he was about to be trampled by celebrating teammates, but it was still meaningful. Later, Orel's mom called it her most meaningful moment of the season. "Just think," she said, "at a time like that, he remembered to thank God."

Another serious concern to the lanky righthander is his family life. He speaks openly of his love for Jamie and their two sons, Orel Leonard Hershiser V ("Quinton") and Jordan. And his love goes beyond words. Once, in 1985, he took the mound a day after little Quinton had fractured his collarbone. O beat the Padres but found himself in tears in the locker room afterward. "I always felt that baseball was a game where you need to stay on an even keel," he explained to puzzled reporters, "but when it comes to family, I am very emotional. You know, first baby, first injury. He's my pride and joy."

Quinton may be Orel's pride and joy—along with recent arrival Jordan—but Jamie is the love of his life. Theirs is a very special relationship. They enjoy taking walks together, seeing good movies and having special dinners, and they regularly attend church together at the Lake Avenue Congregational Church in Pasadena, California. Even while Orel's waiting to bat in the on-deck circle, he always makes it a point to look for Jamie, and talk with her using their own informal sign language.

This kind of closeness is critical for a baseball couple. Otherwise, the frequent separations, and the "groupies," could bring disaster.

"Jamie knows that I've committed my life to her," says the Dodger star. "She does not worry about me when I'm out on the road."

Trust is a key part of any relationship, and Hershiser says their mutual trust is built on the fact that they didn't violate moral standards before marriage. After all, if a couple does have premarital sex, the wife might later be tempted to think, *If he bent the rules before marriage, he might do it again now.*

Says Hershiser, "The perfect plan is to have one wife and not to have sex until you are married. I've found that is fantastic; that is the way to go."

*Congratulations from Dodger manager
Tommy Lasorda on another of Orel's
successful efforts.*
PHOTO: *Andrew D. Bernstein, Los Angeles Dodgers*

But if sex is so fantastic and God is for it (He created it, didn't He?), then why wait until marriage? What's wrong with having sex with a girl, especially if you really love her? Orel notes that sex is not just a physical relationship. "With sex, you're establishing a relationship that is much deeper than a boyfriend-girlfriend commitment. Sex is also mental, emotional and spiritual."

Orel points out that sex can do great damage outside of a permanent commitment. "It's just wrong before marriage," he says. "There's going to be a guilt feeling with it."

O believes that since sex is God's idea, He restricts it to marriage for good reasons. "God knows what He's doing," says the Dodger pitcher. But what reasons does He have for commanding against premarital sex? To protect people from emotional harm and from physical harm (diseases like AIDS) and to prepare them for solid marriages in the future. "I think God puts some boundaries on our lives," says Orel, "but only to protect us from getting hurt and causing hurt. It's just like when you're growing up. When you're a little kid, your parents tell you not to put your hand on a hot burner because you're going to get hurt. Children resist that, but it's for their own good. In the same way, God knows what He's doing with sex. His boundaries are there to protect us and to help us fulfill His eternal plan for us which is to glorify Him and to have fellowship with Him. He's the happiest when I'm the happiest."

Premarital sex, according to Hershiser, is not the way for a teenager to express love. First, he or she needs to learn to communicate with words—an important key for a later sexual relationship in marriage. Second, speaking to young men, Orel observes that real love is patient and sacrificial, not demanding. Thus, a truly loving guy will say, "Because I love you, I'll wait."

But just as obvious as the need for self-control is the fact that it's not easy. What can a young person do to avoid temptation? Orel mentions several principles that have helped him—especially in the big-money, big-pride environment of pro sports.

- *Watch your input.*

  Avoid stimulating material, including pornography but also including lots of the network TV shows and movies.

  "I try to filter those things out," says Orel, "and not expose myself to things I know would be bad for me. When you're exposed to something bad and all of a sudden you realize it, that's when you need to turn away. I've gone to movies and walked out of them."

Hershiser also mentions that the Holy Spirit plays an important role in keeping the Christian from sin.

"When I became a Christian, the Holy Spirit started convicting me of sins. When I walked down the street and saw I was approaching a bar, I sensed the Holy Spirit saying, 'Stay out of there! Stay out of there!' The more I listened to the Holy Spirit, the happier I became and the closer I felt to God."

- *Admit you're weak.*

An honest admission will protect you by reminding you to stay away from wrong situations. If you think you're strong, you will be more likely to find yourself in situations that lead to sin —and that's why the Bible says to "flee youthful lust."

Says Orel, "I stay away from the wrong establishments where I can get into trouble . . . also from the so-called 'groupies' who are around major league teams."

- *Surround yourself with the right kind of people.*

"I'd encourage everyone to get involved with Christian groups and

Christian friends. It's amazing how much you can be strengthened simply by hanging around with people who believe what you believe.

"A lot of people think that Christians don't or can't have fun. That's the stupidest, craziest statement I've ever heard. I was a non-Christian for 21 years, but the years since I became a Christian have been the best of my life."

- *Choose to obey God in every detail of your life.*

Obedience is the key to the sexual area of a person's life as well as other areas.

Says Orel, "Just get up in the morning and say, 'I'm going to say yes to the Holy Spirit today.' That is tough to do, but I've found through spiritual growth that I've learned to say yes to Him more and more. You can't affectionately love God; you can't give Him a big hug; you can't kiss Him. But as it says in the Bible, we show our love for God by obeying Him."

* * *

What a year it was, the 1988 of Orel Hershiser. Consider first the streak, that string of 59 innings without giving up a run. Not only did it break the record held by Don

Drysdale since 1968, but it broke any of the odds or probability tables you might ever see. As *Washington Post* sportswriter Tom Boswell analyzed it, Orel had averaged one shutout in every 11.2 starts preceding his streak. Wrote Boswell: "What are the odds of an 11-to-1 shot coming home six times in a row—i.e., 11 to the sixth power? Our calculator says nearly 2 million to 1." Indeed.

And then there was the rather incredible matter of the 1988 World Series. The Oakland A's swaggered in to the Series, but they didn't swagger out, not the way Orel and the other Dodger pitchers handled the "Bash Brothers" Jose Canseco, Mark McGwire and Dave Parker. Hershiser posted an earned run average of 1.00 for the Series.

"I couldn't figure out why I was missing his pitches in Game 2," said Canseco, who finished 0-for-8 against O. "Then I looked at the videos and I saw how much the ball was moving. In Game 5, I got a good dose of his curveball, which is in Bert Blyleven's class. Great stuff, great pitcher."

Game 2 was especially characteristic of Orel surgery. Hershiser threw a shutout and allowed only three hits, all singles by Parker. And he more than matched Parker's achievement with three hits of his own, a single and two doubles. By now, O was wear-

Concentration: Orel waits for the catcher's next signal.
PHOTO: *Andrew E. Bernstein, Los Angeles Dodgers*

ing out the record keepers as he'd become the first pitcher in 64 years to get three hits in a Series game. "The shutout was satisfying, but the hitting was a thrill," said Hershiser.

But even after all his heroics, Orel still hadn't convinced one of the Oakland hitters—Parker. "Be patient and you can hit him," he told the other A's prior to the fifth and—as it turned out—final game. Parker especially urged his teammates to "lay off that low breaking ball. That's his out pitch."

Poor Parker must still be muttering to himself. Not only did he fail to get a hit, but he struck out on two breaking balls in the dirt (Orel calls them "55-foot curveballs") with two runners on base in the eighth inning.

HERSHISER'S SHUTOUT STREAK

Los Angeles Dodgers' Orel Hershiser set the major league record for consecutive scoreless innings pitched. Hershiser pitched 10 shutout (next page)

Hershiser's 59-inning streak (1988)

Game 1 (Aug. 30): Shut out Montreal in last four innings to begin streak in a 4-2 victory.

Game 2 (Sept. 5): Beat Atlanta 3-0. Struck out eight, walked one, left four men on base.

Game 3 (Sept. 10): Beat Cincinnati 5-0. Struck out eight, gave up seven hits and walked three.

Game 4 (Sept. 14): Beat Atlanta 1-0. Struck out eight, stranded eight baserunners. Los Angeles scored in bottom of the ninth.

Game 5 (Sept. 19): Beat Houston 1-0. Pitched a four-hitter, allowed no walks and left five men on base.

Game 6 (Sept. 23): Beat San Francisco 3-0. Eight consecutive complete games, five hitter. Giants run taken away when Brett Butler was called for interference sliding into second to break up double play.

Game 7 (Sept. 28): Pitched 10 scoreless innings against the San Diego Padres to set record. Left in 11th inning with the score 0-0.

Totals – 59 innings, 36 hits, 11 walks, 43 strikeouts, 36 LOB.

Orel did give up two runs, winning the clinching game, 5-2, but he was super tough when he had to be. Just before striking out Parker in the eighth, and with those same two runners on, Hershiser threw the power-

innings against San Diego to break Los Angeles'
Don Drysdale's record of 58 set in 1968. A game-
by-game look at Hershiser's and Drysdale's
streaks:

Drysdale's 58-inning streak (1968)

Game 1 (May 14): Beat Cubs 1-0 on two hits, three walks, struck out seven.

Game 2 (May 18): Beat Houston 1-0 on five hits, two walks, six strikeouts.

Game 3 (May 22): Beat St. Louis 2-0 on five hits, no walks, eight strikeouts.

Game 4 (May 26): Beat Houston 5-0 on six hits, two walks, six strikeouts.

Game 5 (May 31): Beat San Francisco 3-0 on six hits, two walks, seven strikeouts. Had run erased after he hit Dick Dietz with the bases loaded but call was reversed.

Game 6 (June 4): Beat Pittsburgh 5-0 on three hits, no walks, eight strikeouts.

Game 7 (June 8): Pitched four shutout innings against Philadelphia before Howie Bedell's sacrifice fly in the fifth scored Tony Taylor.

Totals–58 innings, 33 hits, 11 walks, 47 strikeouts, 35 LOB.

ful Canseco an inside fastball. It could have
been an invitation to disaster, but no doubt
Orel was counting on the surprise factor.
Canseco popped out weakly and later said,
"I've never had a guy beat me with fastballs

*Orel stretches to deliver his classic
"55-foot curveball."*
PHOTO: Andrew D. Bernstein, Los Angeles Dodgers

like he did. No excuses . . . he was better."

Hershiser's World Series success gave him major opportunities to relate his faith. Not only did he sing on the Carson show, but he spoke of his love for God when interviewed by NBC's Bob Costas. "I know this isn't a religious show," he told Costas during the locker room celebration, "but I thank God for everything that's happened."

Orel's warmth and sincerity impressed the media. Wrote Bill Reel, a columnist with the *New York Daily News:* "In a time when so many public persons are an embarrassment to themselves and everyone else, we got lucky with a World Series hero who brims with intelligence, cheerfulness, gratitude, openness and, yes, reverence."

What a year it was, but will Orel ever do it again? Can he—could anyone—possibly measure up to the standard he set in 1988?

The swelled-head syndrome shouldn't be a problem, according to Sid Bream, a former Dodger teammate who's now with the Pirates. "He won't change," says Bream. "You can count on it. He's one of the most considerate people I know."

But even with a humble approach, how can Hershiser possibly remain dominant in the highly competitive world of baseball? Sandy Koufax, a pretty fair pitcher in his own day, put this challenge in perspective. "Orel's going to have to get even better, not so much because the rest of the league will catch up to him, but because they're going to want to try that much harder to beat him. He's a remarkable young man and I think he'll get even better."

Orel knows the '88 season has changed his career permanently. "I think my life will be classified in two sections now," he said, "before 1988 and after 1988." Still, he's planning to operate with the same philosophy he's followed before "I'll be the best that I can be," he says. "That's the standard I always set for myself. What the rest of the baseball world sets for me may be something else."

The best that he can be. Yes, slumps are possible and so are injuries, but with Orel Hershiser IV, the best that he can be is marvelously good.

Stay tuned, "Hanes" and "Fruit of the Loom." More T-shirts may soon be needed.

LEAGUE CHAMPIONSHIP SERIES STATISTICS

Year	Club, Opp.	W-L	ERA	G	GS	CG	SHO	SV	IP	H	R	ER	BB	SO
1983	L.A. vs. Phil.					(did not play)								
1985	L.A. vs. St. L.	1-0	3.52	2	2	1	0	0	15.1	17	6	6	6	5
1988	L.A. vs. Mets	1-0	1.09	4	3	1	1	1	24.2	18	5	3	7	15
LCS Totals		2-0	2.03	6	5	2	1	1	40.0	35	11	9	13	20

WORLD SERIES STATISTICS

Year	Club, Opp.	W-L	ERA	G	GS	CG	SHO	SV	IP	H	R	ER	BB	SO
1988	L.A. vs. Oak.	2-0	1.00	2	2	2	1	0	18.0	7	2	2	6	17

ALL-STAR GAME STATISTICS

Year	Club, Site	W-L	ERA	G	GS	CG	SHO	SV	IP	H	R	ER	BB	SO
1987	L.A., Oak.	0-0	0.00	1	0	0	0	0	2.0	1	0	0	1	0
1988	L.A., Cin.	0-0	0.00	1	0	0	0	0	1.0	0	0	0	0	0
ASG Totals		0-0	0.00	2	0	0	0	0	3.0	1	0	0	1	0

LIFETIME NL WON-LOST STATISTICS

W-L	Pct.	vs. Atl.	Chi.	Cin.	Hst.	Mil.	N.Y.	Phil.	Pitt.	St.L.	S.D.	S.F.
83-49	.629	14-6	4-1	11-5	11-5	6-5	3-4	3-4	7-7	5-4	7-4	12-4

MISCELLANEOUS STATISTICS

Year	PITCHING TOTALS					HITTING TOTALS							
	IBB	HB	WP	BK	HR	Avg.	AB	R	H	2B	3B	HR	RBI
1983	0	0	1	0	1	.000	0	0	0	0	0	0	0
1984	8	4	8	1	9	.200	50	4	10	0	0	0	2
1985	5	6	5	0	8	.197	76	5	15	1	0	0	4
1986	11	5	12	3	13	.239	71	4	17	3	0	0	8

BRANCH RICKEY
and
JACKIE ROBINSON

Branch Rickey
and
Jackie Robinson

When Faith Smashed
the Color Barrier

Of all the unusual personalities ever
seen in baseball, no one matches the late
Branch Rickey, Sr.–not Casey Stengel, Leo
Durocher, or George Steinbrenner. Intellec-
tual, philosopher, teacher, religious leader,
Rickey stands alone. This baseball genius
served as chief executive for several teams
between 1917 and 1955, built the sport's first
farm system, introduced sliding pits and bat-
ting tees, emphasized speed, and was one of
the first to urge his players toward "Adventure!" on the basepaths.

The veteran sportswriter Red Smith described Rickey this way: player, manager, executive, lawyer, preacher . . . financier, sociologist, crusader, sharper, father confessor, checker shark, friend and fighter."[1]

Fortunately for baseball, Rickey chose to be different. Without his high ideals and courage the "color barrier" of baseball might have lasted much longer. It's hard to imagine a time when athletic apartheid could have barred Willy Mays or Hank Aaron from organized baseball.

A few blacks played in the big leagues during the 1800s, when the leagues weren't really so big, but by 1892 the color barrier was firmly in place. The Negro Leagues did play the major leaguers in off-season exhibitions, though, and one black player said, "We knew there wasn't any difference because we used to always beat 'em."[2]

Branch Rickey first confronted baseball segregation in 1903 when he began coaching for his college, Ohio Wesleyan University. The team included one black man, Charles Thomas. At the opening of the rookie coach's first game the opposing team players came onto the field, took one look at Thomas, and said they wouldn't play. Rickey walked over to the opponents' bench, pointed a finger at their coach and shouted, "You will play Charles Thomas or you won't play OWU."

He then ordered his players to toss the ball around so they could stay loose. They played catch for an hour before the visitors finally agreed to play. Rickey, only 21 years old, had stood his ground — and he won.

The next season Rickey's OWU team was in South Bend, Indiana, to play Notre Dame. The team had made reservations to stay in the Oliver Hotel, but when the hotel manager saw Charles Thomas in the lobby, he declared that only whites were welcome there. Rickey ordered a cot for Thomas to be put into his own room. "Under no circumstances," he said firmly, "will I leave or allow Thomas to be put out."

Rickey had won another victory, but years later he recalled Thomas's reaction this way: "We went upstairs. I summoned the captain to discuss plans for the game; Tommy stood in the corner, tense and brooding . . . tears spilling down his black face to the floor. Then his shoulders heaved convulsively, and he rubbed one great hand over the other with all the power of his body, muttering, 'Black skin . . . black skin. If I could only make 'em white.' "

Rickey felt the impact of every tear. "For 40 years I've had visions of him trying to wipe off his skin."[3]

Without Charles Thomas in his memory, Branch Rickey may not have been as willing to endure the struggles of the 1940s. But his desire to change baseball's racial climate also came out of his Christian faith.

The Ohio native grew up in a family of deeply committed Christians, and he took the faith into his own heart at an early age. Years later, when tragic headlines shook the world, Rickey had a rock to hold onto. "This will abide," he would say of the Bible.[4]

Rickey's faith influenced his entire life-style (he helped to establish the Fellowship of Christian Athletes), and it eventually led him to set his bespectacled face squarely against segregation in baseball. That's why he made the decision to bring a black player to the Dodgers. He knew, though, that it would take careful planning.

First, the timing. With the end of World War II, when blacks fought side by side with whites, he felt America was finally ready for a change. The people realized the evil they had been battling, Nazi Germany, was based on the faulty idea of one race's superiority.

Second, solid backing. This began to fall into place in the mid-40s when Mr. John L. Smith, another "fervent Christian," became one of the Dodgers' owners.

Third, the right athlete. The man would

History: Jackie Robinson (left) signs with Branch Rickey becoming major league baseball's first black player. PHOTO: UPI

have to be gifted, of course; tough enough to withstand the beanballs and body blocks that would come his way; intelligent, articulate and morally upright so that bigoted critics could not get to first base; and he must be willing to receive abuse without returning it. To fight back would ruin Rickey's "Grand Experiment."

Rickey's scouts found him a player. Of course, this splendid athlete really didn't require much finding. Sports fans in California knew about him. At UCLA, he starred in football, basketball and track as well as in baseball. Twice he led the Pacific Coast Conference (now Pacific 10) in basketball scoring. As a football halfback, he averaged a whopping 11 yards per carry in his junior year and earned All-American honors. In track, he won the National Collegiate Athletic Association championship for the long jump, and he hit .466 one baseball season. His name? Jackie Robinson.

Jackie Robinson had the physical talent to break the color barrier in major league baseball, and he was familiar with racial slurs. At 14, Jackie had gone wading in the Pasadena Reservoir because of a ban against blacks using the municipal pool. Someone saw him splashing and called law enforcement authorities. A few minutes later Jackie was looking at one of the ugliest and most fearful sights of his life: a sheriff pointing a gun at him and yelling, "Looka here. Nigger in my drinking water."[5]

Branch Rickey admired Robinson's strength but he worried about his defiance. Aware that the Army had recently ordered military buses to be desegregated, Lieutenant Jackie Robinson had defied a Southern bus driver's order to sit in the back of the bus. A court martial followed but Jackie was cleared. Yes, he had enough spirit to break baseball's color barrier, but could he walk the emotional tightrope required of a racial pioneer? Or would he lash out in rage and ruin the cause?

The two men met in Rickey's Brooklyn office on August 28, 1945. Robinson thought he was being considered for an all black team, but Rickey stunned him when he said, "I brought you here to play for the Brooklyn Dodgers—if you can!"

The older man asked Jackie if he had a girlfriend and was pleased to hear that the Kansas City Monarch infielder would soon be married. Soon, though, he got to the central point of the interview. Could Robinson keep his cool when fans, opponents or even his own teammates called him a black so-and-so? "Mr. Rickey," answered Jackie, "I think I can play ball, but I promise you that I will do the second part of the job [avoid fights], although I can't be an obsequious, cringing fellow."[6]

With the two-dollar word "obsequious," this UCLA man definitely spoke Rickey's language, and the Dodger was delighted. But he was not yet convinced of Robinson's self-control. Rickey began to portray some of the big league bigots that Robinson would meet.

"Look me in the eye," he said. "Now, I'm a hotel clerk in some lousy dump where they won't like you." His kindly face took on a hard, hateful glare. "You can't stay here," he yelled. "You want to be white? What are you doing this for? Answer me!"

"I don't want to be white," replied Jackie. "I just want to play big league ball."

Next, Rickey portrayed a young tough, perhaps an opposing player. "A nigger is a nigger and that's all he'll ever be—just a nigger," he roared. "Well, what've you got to say?" As Robinson began to answer, Rickey kicked him in the shin.

Jackie's eyes lit with anger; his fists clenched. Rickey later said he wondered if an attack might follow.

But then Robinson dropped his hands. "I don't want to make any trouble," he said to the "young tough." "I just came here to play ball."[7]

"Suppose," said Rickey, "a player comes down from first base—you are the shortstop—the player slides, spikes high, and cuts you on the leg. As the blood runs down your leg, the white player laughs in your face, and sneers, 'How do you like that, nigger boy?' "

Robinson asked Rickey, "Are you looking for a Negro who is afraid to fight back?"

"I'm looking for a ballplayer with guts enough *not* to fight back!" Rickey reached into his desk drawer and brought out *The Life of Christ* by Giovanni Papini, an Italian once famous as an atheist but one who had experienced a stunning conversion. Rickey quietly began to read some famous words of Jesus from Matthew 5 and Papini's related comments:

> *"Ye have heard that it hath been said, An eye for an eye, and a tooth for a tooth: But I say unto you, that ye resist not evil: But whosoever shall smite thee on the right cheek, turn to him the other also . . . "*

> Every man has an obscure respect for courage in others, especially if it is moral courage, the rarest and most difficult sort of bravery . . . the results of nonresistance, even if they are not always perfect, are certainly superior to those of resistance or flight . . . To answer blows with blows, evil deeds with evil deeds, is to meet the attacker on his own ground, to proclaim oneself as low as he . . . Only he who has conquered himself can conquer his enemies.

Rickey laid the book down. "Now," he said to Robinson, "you will have to promise that for the first three years in baseball you will turn your other cheek. Three years — can you do it?"

"Mr. Rickey," said Jackie Robinson, "I've got two cheeks. Is that it?"[8]

On October 23, 1945, Jackie Robinson

signed a contract for the '46 season to play with Brooklyn's top farm team, the Montreal Royals. Rickey felt Robinson could use a year to prepare, physically and mentally, for the big leagues. It proved to be a good move. Canadians, somewhat removed from the racial problems of America, quickly received Robinson as a hero. However, Jackie's manager, a Southerner named Clay Hopper, was not such an instant admirer.

Rickey saw Hopper's initial reaction to Robinson during a spring training game. "In the seventh inning, Jackie (playing second base) made one of those tremendous plays that very few people can make . . . I put my hand on Clay's shoulder and said, 'Did you ever see a play to beat it?' Now this fellow comes from Greenwood, Mississippi. And he shook me [with] his face that far from me, and he said, 'Do you really think that a nigger is a human being, Mr. Rickey?' I never answered him."[9]

Nor did Rickey need to. "Six months later he came into my office after the year in Montreal. 'I want to take back what I said to you last spring,' he said. 'I'm ashamed of it. Now, you may have plans for Robinson to be on your Brooklyn club, but if you don't I would like to have him back at Montreal. He is not only a great ballplayer, good enough for Brooklyn, but he is also a fine gentle-man.' "10

A perfect gentleman he was in Mon-treal, but Robinson was not kind to oppos-ing pitchers. He topped the International League in hitting (.349 average) and in runs scored (113), and with his teammates won the Little World Series to become the cham-pions of the minor leagues.

Jackie was ready for the Dodgers. But both he and Rickey knew that the 1947 sea-son would be the greatest challenge of their lives. Could Jackie hold up under the con-stant abuse he would receive? Could Rickey, in his mid-60s by now and suffering from Meniere's Disease, cope with reporters' at-tacks and also support Robinson?

The first major test came from within Dodger ranks. Several of the players signed a petition stating they would not play for Brooklyn if a black man did. The movement might have become a major threat except for Pee Wee Reese. A native Kentuckian who probably never had shaken a black man's hand, Reese was expected to side with Jack-ie's foes. But for financial reasons he chose not to. He later became Robinson's closest friend on the team–and his golfing buddy.

The next tests were to come from oppos-ing teams. For example, the Phillies' general manager said he feared a riot by fans if Robinson came with the Dodgers to play in Philadelphia. He told Rickey, "We won't be able to take the field with your Brooklyn team if that boy Robinson is in uniform."

Rickey was ready with a firm reply. "If we must claim the game 9-0 [the score for any forfeit], we will do just that, I assure you," he said.[11]

The Phillies played, but, led by their manager, they yelled ugly things about Robinson and his wife, and they told the other Dodgers not to touch Jackie's towels or comb if they wanted to avoid disease.

By this time some of the Dodgers who had once opposed Jackie now found themselves admiring his quiet strength and began defending him, yet problems persisted. News that the St. Louis Cardinals might boycott their games with the Dodgers got out and National League President Ford Frick told Cardinal owner Sam Braedon to tell his players that "this is America and baseball is America's game. Tell them that if they go on strike for racial reasons . . . they will be barred from baseball even though it means the disruption of a club or a whole league."[12] You guessed it–no strike in St. Louis.

And the death threats–Robinson was receiving so many of them that Rickey finally had the Dodger office open all his mail.

The first season took a heavy toll on both Rickey and Robinson. Rickey got flak from many other baseball executives — and plenty of hate mail. As a result, he was troubled more than ever by his disease. Despite his own problems, though, Rickey and his wife Jane invited the Robinsons to their home, took them on picnics, and reminded them from the Bible of Job's patience during trials.

The eventual victory soon became obvious, both in Jackie's performance and in the fan response. He hit .297 that first season, led the league in stolen bases ("Adventure!"), won the Rookie of the Year award and helped take the Dodgers to the World Series where it took seven games for the Yankees to defeat them. Following successes brought Jackie the Most Valuable Player award in 1949, when he hit .342; and a World Series crown for the Dodgers in 1955. As for the fans, both white and black responded to him. A national poll taken at the end of 1947 revealed him to be one of America's most popular figures, second only to Bing Crosby.[13]

So the "Grand Experiment" proved to be a grand slam success. Other blacks followed Robinson to the Dodgers, and Larry Doby signed with Cleveland, the first black in the American League. Seven years before the Supreme Court outlawed segregation in America's schools, many major league teams had at least one black player.

Rickey was thrilled. "God was with me when I picked Jackie," he said. "I don't think any other man . . . could have done what he did those first two or three years."[14]

Robinson never did stop expressing his sincere thanks to his Dodger boss. He said, "I really believe that in breaking down the color barrier in baseball, our 'national game,' he did more for the Negroes than any white man since Abraham Lincoln."[15]

Rickey frequently reminded people that his Christian faith had moved him to sign Robinson. That makes sense when you read what he wrote in his 20s: "Power to make others happy is the greatest asset in the world, I think. We must believe in the doctrine of 'Loving God and one's brothers.' Jesus Christ made people happy just by loving them."[17]

The conclusion is simple. Jackie Robinson's courage broke baseball's color barrier. Branch Rickey's Christian faith in action gave him his chance. Baseball owes them both a great debt.

BOBBY
RICHARDSON

The former Yankee second baseman made history with a World Series grand slam. He enjoys telling the story – and using it to inspire others.

Bobby Richardson

My Grand Slam and Yours

Bobby Richardson was never known for power hitting, unless perhaps the lack of it. In the Yankee lineup of the 1950s and 1960s, he was the one who didn't hit home runs, in contrast to such sluggers as Mickey Mantle, Roger Maris and Yogi Berra. Richardson instead helped the New Yorkers build a dynasty with his fine fielding and his hit-and-run ability.

But Richardson must have used somebody else's bat in the third game of the 1960

World Series against the Pirates. In the first inning, he belted a grand slam; then he knocked in two more runs in the fourth. His 6 runs-batted-in for the game and 12 for the Series both set new records. Although the Pirates won the championship, Richardson was named Most Valuable Player.

Retired as a player since 1966, Richardson is baseball coach at Liberty University (Lynchburg, Virginia) and is president of Baseball Chapel.

* * *

No one was more surprised than I was when that ball flew out of Yankee Stadium for a grand slam in the third World Series game of 1960. Why? To start with, I'd hit only one home run that entire season. Next, I went to the plate with instructions to squeeze bunt, and it was only after I'd fouled off two pitches that I was allowed to swing away. Even then, however, I was just trying to hit the ball to the right side to keep from hitting into a double play.

Fortunately, I swung a little early at Clem Labine's pitch, and the ball headed toward the left fielder. When I rounded first base, I looked toward left field for the first time. Gino Cimoli had already gone to the fence and was looking down into his glove. I thought he had caught the ball, and there was a little sinking feeling in my heart.

Cimoli was looking into an empty glove. The ball had cleared the wall, and I experienced one of the top thrills of my career. I'll never forget circling the bases and then being greeted by three teammates who had also scored on just one swing of the bat. And to think that I was supposed to have bunted!

Not every grand slam takes place in a World Series game, but every grand slam is a breathtaking event. The impact of four runs on one play is overwhelming in a Little League or high school game just as in a big league game.

And that's why I'd like to describe an experience I've had in the Christian life by calling it a "spiritual grand slam." Allow me to tell you more about the time I personally received Jesus Christ as my Savior and Lord.

As a small boy, I went to church and Sunday school and memorized a lot of Scripture verses. I knew all about the story of Jesus Christ, but I did not know Him personally. One afternoon, at age 14, I talked with my pastor and suddenly realized that real Christianity didn't mean just living a good life. It meant that I must receive Christ as Lord and Savior of my life. So, that day I invited Christ into my life.

I call that experience a spiritual grand slam because it was the greatest event in my life. It introduced me to a God who loves me despite my weaknesses, who forgives my sins, who promises me eternal life. I simply cannot imagine going through life without His friendship and strength. I'm sure the players who are profiled in this book would say the same. Fortunately, this same experience of knowing Christ personally can be shared by anyone who responds in faith to the following truths.

- *First, a spiritual grand slam is based on your awareness of God's love.*

What kind of love does He have for you? An unconditional love, one that flows from Him regardless of your actions or attitudes. As the Bible puts it, "But God demonstrates His own love toward us, in that while we were yet sinners, Christ died for us" (Romans 5:8). It's also a love that has no limit. I say this because God was willing to send His own Son to die for us—that's how much He loves us. "For God so loved the world that He gave His only begotten Son, that whoever believes in Him should not perish but have eternal life" (John 3:16).

- *Second, a spiritual grand slam involves an understanding of sin.*

If you packed 50,000 people into Yankee

Stadium, you could be sure that every single one of the 50,000 was sinful. How do I know? The Bible says, "All have sinned and fall short of the glory of God" (Romans 3:23). The result of sin is serious, to say the least. According to the Bible, "The wages of sin is death" (Romans 6:23). Our sins bring with them a bitter payment—eternal separation from God—unless we find forgiveness.

- *Third, a spiritual grand slam requires an answer to the sin problem.*

Fortunately, we are not required to supply that answer ourselves. That is what Jesus did when He died on the cross. Simply put, He took upon Himself our sins and accepted the wages for those sins through His own death (see Matthew 20:28 and 1 Peter 2:24). He rose again three days after His death, thus proving that He was and is the Son of God.

- *Fourth, a spiritual grand slam is possible only when we respond in faith to Jesus Christ.*

We cannot reach God simply by attending church or doing good deeds, for these efforts cannot erase our sins. Instead, we must depend completely on Jesus for forgiveness. As the Bible says, "For by grace you have been saved through faith; and that not of yourselves, it is the gift of God; not as a result of works" (Ephesians 2:8,9). In order to know Christ, a person must receive Him by faith. The Bible says, "But as many as received Him, to them He gave the right to become children of God, even to those who believe in His name" (John 1:12). Before I ever put on those Yankee pinstripes, I had to sign a contract with the team. The same is true with God—to be part of His family we each must make a clear-cut decision to trust Christ as Savior and Lord.

Perhaps you're wondering how you can be sure that Christ will respond to your faith. How will you know that He has forgiven you and come into your life? No, He won't necessarily give you the kind of goose-bumps that go along with a grand slam in baseball. Instead, He offers something more reliable than emotions—His own promise to live within the heart of those who receive Him by faith. As Jesus said, "Behold, I stand at the door and knock; if anyone hears My voice and opens the door, I will come in to him" (Revelation 3:20).

If you understand and believe the things you've just read, I would suggest that you now trust Jesus to be your personal Savior. You can express your faith in prayer, which is simply talking with God. Your prayer should include the following thoughts:

1. Admit you are a sinner.
2. Thank God for sending His Son, Jesus Christ, to pay the penalty for your sins by dying on the cross.
3. Accept His forgiveness for your sins.
4. Ask Jesus to come into your life.
5. Express your willingness to allow Him to change your life so that you might live in a way that honors Him.

Why don't you take a minute right now to pray these things to God? This spiritual grand slam is a once-in-a-lifetime commitment, so make sure that you understand clearly what you've just read.

* * *

Did you pray those thoughts to God with faith and sincerity? If you did, Jesus Christ entered your heart, bringing with Him forgiveness for your sins. You may or may not feel any different, but that's not important. Your new relationship with God is based on what Christ promised, not on how you feel.

If you did trust Jesus to be your Savior, you will soon observe changes in your attitudes and actions. As you have seen in Orel Hershiser's story, these changes may affect your attitude toward yourself, your attitude toward relatives and friends, and even your purpose for life. (See 2 Corinthians 5:17.)

One final word. Just as any ballplayer functions best on a good team, so a Christian is strong only as a part of a fellowship group. Make sure to become part of a church where Christ is honored and the Bible is clearly explained. The people in such a church can show you Christ's love and teach you how to follow Him.

I would also invite you to write to me so that I can send you materials to aid your spiritual growth. Please don't hesitate.

I still remember the joy of my spiritual grand slam, and I'm eager to share in yours! Please write to:

Bobby Richardson
c/o Here's Life Publishers
P. O. Box 1576
San Bernardino, CA 92402-1576

NOTICE

Would you like a number of these
Orel Hershiser booklets
for your church youth group,
baseball club, or other organization?

Discounts are available on
large quantity orders
for such organizations.

For further information,
call Here's Life Publishers
toll-free at
1-800-950-4HLP.